As Winter Melts into Spring...

...we begin waiting patiently for the signs of vibrant new life. Our senses are tuned to the subtle changes around us—longer days, the gradual warming of the sun's rays, the sight and sounds of the first birds returning from their migrations, the steady retreat of a season's worth of shimmering snow.

There is wonder in this time of year, just before spring arrives. We know that unseen pastel blossoms and brilliant green leaves are already beginning to stir, and we eagerly await their stunning annual display.

It's a season of wonder...and waiting...and patience.

Fred Sieb

Come, Spend *A Year in the Country*

THERE'S nothing like a leisurely walk through the countryside to lift your spirits and make you feel at ease. The beauty of the changing seasons is something you shouldn't let slip by unnoticed.

That's why we're proud to unveil our fourth—and best yet—edition of *A Year in the Country*. Inside, you'll find a whole year's worth of visits to rural America compiled into one gorgeous coffee-table book ...so you can take a trip through the country whenever you like—without leaving your favorite chair!

Simply take a moment and "stroll" through the following pages. Each glossy, gloriously-rich photo offers a wake-up call for the senses—*see* each season unfold before your eyes...*smell* spring's floral

Steve Terrill

scents...*feel* summer's hazy heat...*taste* autumn's juicy harvest...and *hear* the wintry winds whistling outside. From the first blossom of spring to the final frosty leaf fluttering down, each photo's so vivid you'll feel like you're actually *there*!

Linger awhile and read the inspirational stories and poems, each written by folks who love country living as much as you do. This book's breathtaking photos, whimsical poetry and heartwarming prose can make the country seem near and dear even to people who aren't fortunate to live there.

So, take a trip along rural back roads with us. Curl up in your favorite chair and enjoy *A Year in the Country*.

Printed in U.S.A.
International Standard Book Number: 0-89821-095-X
Library of Congress Catalog Card Number: 91-62330

Publisher: Roy Reiman
Editor: Linda Piepenbrink
Publications Editor: Bob Ottum
Art Director: Jim Sibilski
Art Associate: Stephanie Marchese
Production: Sally Manich
           Ellen Lloyd

Cover photo by Doyle Yoder; back cover by Henry J. Hupp/ Laatsch-Hupp Photo.

A YEAR IN THE Country

David Stoecklein

Saddle Up 'n Join Us for Super Scenery on Horseback!

THE COWBOY has long been an American hero. Many of us envy his freedom, rugged life on the land, and steady diet of adventure.

Why would a man spend his life in the middle of nowhere? As Charlie Daniels says it in song, "Don't ask that question unless you've topped a hill at first light and seen the dew diamonds sparkling in a thousand-acre pasture...or smelled the sage stomped out of horses' hooves...or tasted old Cookie's coffee.

"Don't judge him until you've watched calves kicking up their heels, or heard the squeak of saddle leather. Come sit by my fire, ride my gentlest horse, sleep under my stars, and drink from my mountain streams..."

Until that opportunity presents itself, settle for riding with us through these pages. Saddle up and join us for a horseback view of the American West. And then maybe, just maybe, you'll understand why—for a real cowboy—no other way of life will do.

DAY STARTS EARLY for Colorado cowboy as he shoulders saddle and lariats in preparation for another long day of roundup.

David Stoecklein

PLAINS COWBOY (above) closes in on cold day in Utah. At right, ranch hand sizes up one of latest additions to herd, a range-born calf still unsteady on wobbly knees.

WILD HORSES (left) kick up spray as they thunder into a stream during a roundup near Mackay, Idaho, with the majestic Lost River mountain range a breathtaking backdrop.

SUN SETS SLOWLY (lower right) as cowboy makes his final rounds on Montana ranch. The work is demanding, but the rewards—like this sunset—can't be topped.

WYOMING WRANGLER (below) waits patiently as horses take a welcome break from their work for a drink of cool, refreshing water on ranch in Colter Bay, Wyoming.

H. Armstrong Roberts

Roy Marshall

David Stoecklein

10

MILLING CATTLE graze contentedly, above, on wind-swept landscape in the Upper Plains. Lone cowboy keeps a watchful eye on the charges and his spacious scenery.

OWNER'S PRIDE is evident in burnished saddle (far left). South Dakota horseman oils it regularly to keep it gleaming and to highlight its intricate hand-tooled detailing.

ROUNDUP PROCEEDS at a relaxed, leisurely trot as cowboys at left herd even-tempered spotted horses through scenic Sawtooth Mountain range in south-central Idaho.

UNTAMED STALLION bucks vigorously (upper right) as cowboy lassoes him and starts to rein him in. Action took place during wild horse roundup near Missoula, Montana.

"CHOW TIME!" Camp cook on ranch in the Northwest clangs chime to summon cowboys back for hearty noontime meal. Judging from his broad grin, a fine feast must be in store!

BEAUTY SURROUNDS rider pausing quietly with his dog and pack mule, taking in panoramic view and watching shadows lengthen on Northwest mountain range.

THUNDERING HOOVES stir up clouds of snow as bundled-up cowboy drives wild horses across frost-encrusted range land in High Plains.

COZY CAMP FIRE warms cowboys on roundup, far left, as they prepare meal on edge of steep ridge overlooking snow-capped mountain peaks.

LITTLE COWPOKE watches carefully —taking mental notes for the day he's big enough for *his* turn—as his father shoes a horse in Mackay, Idaho.

TURN THE PAGE to share a serene view with Steve Bush and his Appaloosa as they ride into Snake River canyon near Pomeroy, Washington.

"Wake up," whispered Winter,
Pretending to be Spring,
"Don't you want to be the first
To hear the robins sing?"
So up popped a yellow crocus
From its bed, secure and warm…
Just in time to see that tease
Laughing up a storm.
—*Dona Maddux Cooper, Stillwater, Oklahoma*

Rick Miller

Mountain Memory Gives Peace to Coach's Pace

Cherished reflection of an isolated
mountain lake calms the spirit of this Olympic coach.

By Bill Neville, Santee, California

MY JOB as head coach of the U.S. men's volleyball team takes me to large cities around the world. When I'm assailed by the crowds, noises and smells of urban life, I take "time out" for a trip back to the country…in my memory.

No matter where I am, I can always transport myself back to one glorious spring day in southwestern Montana.

I was living in Bozeman then, and had accompanied my sister—she's a forest ranger—as she set out on horseback into the Gravelly Range of the Rocky Mountains.

It was a crisp pre-dawn morning. While my sister made notes in her field book, I rode my horse up toward a distant ridge to watch the sun rise.

As I slowly worked the horse along a bubbling brook that threaded its way through the verdant forest, I came upon what appeared to be fresh elk tracks. I was curious and followed them.

As the sun began to rise, I traced the elk trail to the top of the ridge, which was carpeted with wild flowers, spotted with rock outcroppings and accented with winter ever-

greens. All around me, the peaceful forest and snow-capped peaks stood tall against a cloudless sky.

Finally I reached the crest of the ridge, and from there, looked down on the most beautiful sight I had ever seen—a herd of elk making its way toward the edge of a turquoise lake. The water was still and as smooth as a mirror, reflecting the towering, snow-dappled spires behind it.

The elk looked up at me, but gave me no more than a passing appraisal, then went about their early-morning ritual with ease and elegance.

At first I scolded myself for not bringing my camera. Then I thought, "No. This scene, this moment, will be in my mind forever. I'll keep it available for instant recall anytime I choose."

Now, whenever my job in some far-off "civilized" place becomes too serious or tense, I call up that scene in my mind's eye.

And I smile to myself, knowing that when I am done with this task, I will take time to return to that isolated spot on a ridge in Montana to "recharge" myself again.

Spring Creeps in...Softly, Quietly, Colorfully

CONSIDER this a minute: Would spring be as popular if it didn't follow winter?

Maybe the reason we love it so—at least those of us in Northern states—is that we've anticipated it for so long, while enduring snow, ice, cold and slush.

After 3 to 4 months of that, we're ready for a *change.* Any change! Unfortunately, while spring has a lot going for it, it sure takes its good time getting here. Sometimes we're fully convinced the season forgot us completely, and that we'll go direct from winter to summer. And then, just as you've given up on it, it sneaks in overnight. One morning you notice that trees have silently sprouted delicate buds, wild flowers have sent up tender shoots, and there's a bird out back you haven't seen for a while.

Next thing you know, the season springs up everywhere. And that's when you take a long look, a good deep breath, and conclude once again it was worth the wait.

SWALLOWTAIL BUTTERFLY (right) stops for sip of nectar in Slippery Rock, Penn., its colorful wings rivaling the flower's beauty.

BLOSSOMS ENHANCE the rustic surroundings of this well-kept Clinton Mill in rural New Jersey.

CARPET OF POPPIES (at left) is reflected in artist's rendering of California's Antelope Valley. She'll save scene to enjoy again and again!

MULTI-HUED AZALEAS in magenta, white and fuchsia line an inviting path through thick woods (below) in Orangeburg, South Carolina.

Ken DeQuaine

TULIP TIME arrives in carefully tended garden (above) near Leland, Wisconsin.

Don Shenk

Fred Sieb

Willard Clay

Ken DeQuaine

SERENE SCENE (above) surrounds lone boater on placid, azalea-bordered Mountain Creek Lake near Pine Mountain, Georgia.

HONEYBEE HOVERS over a delectable blossom (far left) in Lancaster, Pennsylvania, where bee's arrival is sure sign of spring!

BRIGHT BLOSSOMS of plants growing wild or put there by caring person add color to covered bridge (far left) at Conway, N.H.

PRETTY PETALS of bold sunflowers (left) offset delicate Queen Anne's lace along an isolated rural road in Carroll County, Illinois.

ROBIN RETURNS to California's Sacramento Valley (right) and surveys his domain from branches of apricot tree in early bloom.

Ron Sanford

21

Steve Terrill

H. Armstrong Roberts

Jerry Jacka

Larry Ulrich

COLORFUL FLOWERS (above), including marigolds, black-eyed Susans, zinnias and pansies, enhance the beauty of secluded barn near Grand Ronde, Oregon.

VIBRANT NEW LIFE springs forth from an Eastern redbud tree (far left) in northern Missouri as first tender green leaves emerge amid a riot of soft pink blossoms.

LUSH EVERGREENS are complemented by purple and yellow flowers on the Red Mountain Pass (left) alongside Highway 550 outside Silverton, Colorado.

SAND VERBENA and evening primrose flourish prettily in the sandy soil at the foot of Coyote Mountain, which is located in southern California's Borrego Desert State Park.

TURN THE PAGE for a dazzling springtime scene overlooking Yankee Bay Basin in the Colorado Rockies. The snow-capped peaks and the basin are seen from the road to Mountain Top Mine near Ouray, Colorado.

Jerry Jacka

Springtime Sparks Memories of Watching Willows Grow

A father's faith turned two spindly branches into the childhood sanctuary of his daughters' dreams.

By Juanita Daniel Zachry, Abilene, Texas

Barbara Laatsch-Hupp/Laatsch-Hupp Photo

WHEN the willows bloom in early spring, I'm always reminded of my girlhood days on the farm.

Years ago, soon after our big white farmhouse was built, Dad planted numerous trees—poplars, silver-leaf maples, lilacs and crepe myrtles—on three sides. Then he turned his attention to the back yard, where the brook crossed.

"A willow tree would be just the thing," he said. "No …*two*—there's space for two."

Our mother protested. "Not willows," she said. "A mulberry can grow in that space instead and provide much nicer shade."

"But willows grow fast," Dad said. "And they're easy to propagate."

"They need lots of water," Mother pointed out.

"The brook will take care of that," Dad countered. "And if it floods, they'll help hold back the creek!"

Mother sighed and went into the house. Dad grinned and motioned for me and my sister, Millie, to follow him down to the marsh. There he cut two slender willow branches about 3 feet long. Back in our yard, he pushed half their length in the moist soil by the brook.

Not long after, the first tender sprouts burst forth…and from then on those willows grew *fast*.

The next summer, Dad pruned the new willow trees and transplanted them closer to the brook, about 8 feet apart. "Soon you'll be playing under them," he promised Millie and me. We watched their progress, and even while they were small, we considered them our special trees.

Eventually, those spindly branches grew into trees more than 30 feet tall, with sturdy, 2-foot trunks! Later, Millie and I loved to stretch our small arms around the trunks, trying to get our fingers to touch, but we never could.

The low, curving branches created a private sanctuary that soon became our playhouse. Our willow canopy was a haven for make-believe; it could be anything we imagined —a corral, a school or a church. We loved darting in and out of the branches' shelter during gentle showers, squealing with delight as scattered raindrops tickled us.

Mother (who'd soon forgotten her preference for mulberry trees) often brought us picnic lunches under the willows. She'd spread a red checked cloth on the ground, and we'd enjoy our lunch with streaks of sunlight crisscrossing our faces.

Finally, Millie and I outgrew our willow playhouse. But I'll never outgrow my love of those trees—especially in spring, when their glorious array of spiraling branches are edged in tiny, greenish-yellow flowers.

Some folks say willows weep. But whenever I see a willow, I remember…and *smile*.

Friendly Fawn Frames Photographer's Dreams

Sometimes, as this photographer learned,
life's greatest pleasures are the ones that take us by surprise!

Story and photo by Len Holland, Birmingham, Alabama

ALL PHOTOGRAPHERS dream of that "once-in-a-lifetime" photo opportunity…and all too often when it comes, they've left their camera behind!

That happened to me recently during a camping trip in the Great Smoky Mountains of North Carolina. But—amazingly—I got a second chance.

I'd camped in the Cataloochee Valley and I had it mostly to myself—there were few other tourists braving the early-spring chill. I got up before dawn for a walk, thinking about the photos I planned to take later and hoping I would be able to photograph some deer.

The air was still, broken only by the night sounds of the forest and the babbling of a small brook.

As I walked along in the dark, I suddenly felt something nudge the back of my leg, much the way a dog might nudge its owner. A shiver ran down my back. What was it? A dog? A bear? I felt another nudge and decided, like it or not, it was time to find out.

Flashlight in hand, I took two long, quick steps forward, then whirled to shine the light in the creature's eyes, hoping to startle it and give me a chance to get away.

But the light showed nothing; it was aimed too high. I lowered the beam…and stared into the face of a fawn!

I thought of my three children and how wonderful it would have been to have them see this beautiful creature close-up. All this beauty—and I didn't have my camera!

I lifted my hand toward the fawn, thinking he probably would run. But he just stood there, letting me pet him and rub his head and neck!

After a few minutes, I turned off the flashlight and started walking, sure the fawn would vanish into the night. Instead, he followed me along the road, nudging the back of my leg now and then to ask for another pat!

Then, just as suddenly as it had appeared, the fawn was gone. I searched the edge of the woods with my flashlight, but there was no trace of it anywhere.

I was sorry I didn't have my camera, but I was grateful for the experience, and eager to tell my family about it when I got home.

The next morning I was in a quiet area of the valley about a mile away, photographing the sunrise. I was startled by a rustling in the bushes. It was the fawn again! And this time I had my camera!

The fawn again came right up to me and let me pet and photograph him. He got so close to me that I had to clean the camera lens *twice* because he kept sticking his nose into it!

As the morning light grew stronger and the sun began to warm the valley, the fawn meandered away, walking into the woods for the last time.

I still don't know why the fawn ignored his instincts and approached me, but I'm glad he did. He gave me the chance to photograph one of nature's most gentle creatures, and to share his beauty with others. It was a wonderful experience, and one I won't soon forget!

Julie Habel

May's 'Blackberry Drizzle' Makes a Sweet Remembrance

Julie Habel

For those who grew up in the country, the sweetest childhood memories often are the simplest.

By Janey Ashlene, Miami, Florida

Every time I see pretty rows of jams and jellies in the grocery, I think of the month of May, kerosene rags and my grandmother's wonderful blackberry preserves.

When I was growing up in Kentucky, there was always one week in May when the newly warmed air got a damp chill, and a fine, misty drizzle would fall for several days. Old-timers called it the "blackberry drizzle" or "blackberry winter", because that was the week that the wild blackberry bushes would bloom.

Our anticipation began to build that week as the briars changed from dark green vines with stickers into thorny greenery, covered with sweet-smelling white sprays of flowers. We knew that blackberry picking time was only weeks away!

Later, when the berries ripened, the women and girls would prepare for our "blackberry outing". And it took plenty of preparation!

We started by tearing an old sheet into strips, which we soaked in kerosene and tied around our wrists and ankles to keep out the chiggers (mite-sized insects). Then we'd don long-sleeved pants and shirts, and tie the pant legs with twine. After completing our costumes with straw hats or sunbonnets, we were ready to head out to the pastures.

The wild blackberry bushes were lovely when the fruit ripened. The berries at the end of each drooping branch ripened first, into clusters of soft, shiny, purple-black fruit, just waiting for your hand to catch them as they fell. Farther back on the branch, the berries ripened more slowly and turned a luscious red that matched the color of the leaves' edges.

I always knew I'd picked a good berry by the sound it made when it hit my small quart pail. If it landed with a soft *thunk* that sounded as if it might have squashed, it was a good one. The berries that made a *plink* would have a sharp, bitter taste.

Often I was accused of eating more than I put in my pail, but that wasn't always the case. It just seemed that the largest, shiniest, ripest berry on the end of each thorny green branch needed to be tested to see if it tasted as good as it looked!

There were hazards, though. The kerosene rags didn't do much to head off chiggers. We always counted our bites afterward, and anyone with fewer than 25 was considered lucky! "Sweat bees" always seemed to find me out there, too. And I often had to stop to pluck the blackberry thorns out of my legs.

We also had to watch for "cow pats", although Grandma always laughed at that and said it was nicer to call them "cow roses". Still, no matter what you called them, you had to watch where you stepped!

All those hazards were forgotten by afternoon, when the smell of blackberries filled our homes as the fruit was preserved and baked into pies. Grandma's preserves always tasted better than anyone's.

Each time I visited her house later on, Grandma would fetch me a jar of preserves from her fruit cellar. I always ate a spoonful straight from the jar, just to see if it was as good as I'd remembered. It was.

Those pretty pots of jam and jellies I see in the grocery these days never taste as sweet. But they always take me back to those simpler days that started each May with "blackberry drizzle".

The Garden Path

By Marlene Feulner Norcross
Magna, Utah

I TOOK TIME today to walk along the garden path—to meditate, to fantasize, to daydream.

The garden path is a world removed from schedules, clocks and telephones. It is a place where there are no demands—no need to respond, to react, or be all things to all people.

As I plucked the flowers that had overcome the weeds —just as good times had overcome the bad in my life —I thought of what had been, what is, and what will be.

It is here that I discover who I am and where I am going.

Everyone needs a garden path in his or her life—a place for meditation and inspiration, where all is right with the world and one is at peace.

Blossoming Barnyard

*Spring is in full swing!
Countless clusters of budding apple blossoms
and grass loaded with colorful dandelions frame
an inviting red barn at a farm
near Ponemah, New Hampshire.*

Springtime's Special to Country Kids!

Now that spring's here, country kids can't wait to get outside and revel in it, as these reader photos prove!

It's a great time of year for rural youngsters to learn more about the world around them. Everything seems fresh and new, from the blooming tulips to the cuddly new animals just waiting for a little bit of tender loving care.

The kids pictured here obviously are enjoying everything spring has to offer. Hope you are, too!

"MY TURN!" Courtney Brown of Sandy, Utah loves playing with family dog, Carmel. "Ball" was even her first word!

PUPPY LOVE. Andrew Tyler of Aurora, Ind. found willing pals when family's Golden Retriever gave birth to 10 pups!

PETTABLE PIGLETS. Matthew Morovic of Freeport, Ill. gingerly pets newborn pigs on his aunt and uncle's farm. Mom Kayla was there to record the meeting!

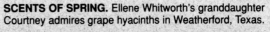

SCENTS OF SPRING. Ellene Whitworth's granddaughter Courtney admires grape hyacinths in Weatherford, Texas.

"WOW!" Zeke Schupp is wild about strawberries, says Grandma Joan Heisel of Labadie, Mo. We believe her!

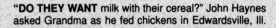

"DO THEY WANT milk with their cereal?" John Haynes asked Grandma as he fed chickens in Edwardsville, Ill.

"I'LL TAKE THIS ONE!" Jacob Schroeder of Coffeyville, Kansas wanted a bouquet for Mom, but had to shake off a bug first!

COUNTRY KITTENS. Angelea Rene Busby of Lenexa, Kansas cuddles kittens on visit to cousins' farm in rural Missouri.

Get Ready...
Here Comes Summer!

Remember those early spring days that reminded you more of winter...when the sky was gray, the grass was brown and the cold nights left you feeling blue?

Well, remember no more, because the woods have awakened with the fresh scents and sights of summer. There are budding trees to behold, flowers to unfold and sunsets made of shimmering gold.

So take time...make time...to "stop and smell the roses" and enjoy summer to the fullest!

Farm 'Crick' Was Center Of Child's Summer World

By Jo Carey, Skwentna, Alaska

❖

I CALLED IT Lick Crick. During my girlhood in Indiana, the stream meandered gently along the edge of our farm, and in summer it was the center of my little world.

My time at the crick would start in May, when Daddy and I would dig a canful of wiggly worms and walk to the grassy bank for some fishing. We'd spend hours there, contentedly sitting side by side.

All we ever caught were silver dollar-sized sunfish and an occasional crawdad. It didn't matter—the thrill wasn't in catching a big one, but in watching the bobber bob and yanking in a fish of *any* size.

Daddy cleaned them all, no matter how small, and Mother fried them for supper. Every bite-sized morsel was savored and remembered.

Come June, I'd dodge buzzing swarms of bees as I gathered perfumed blossoms from the black locust trees that lined the bank and shaded the water. The honey-sweet, creamy white blooms dripped in heavy, fragrant clusters from the branches.

In the humid, sweltering days of July and August, I'd "swim". The water came up to my waist—if I sat down. I'd sit in the cool stream, raising my feet just enough so the ripples carried me along, bouncing from one rocky seat to the next. When I lost my balance and fell back, the water trickled, clean and refreshing, over my head.

Then came the lazy weekends of September. School had started, and days had the nip of autumn. Swimming no longer was inviting. But still Lick Crick beckoned.

After chores were completed on Saturdays and church was over on Sundays, I ran to the leaning tree below the towering old iron bridge. The gnarled maple had grown in two sections, and the twin trunks arched away from each other in such a way as to make a fairly comfortable "couch". The back rest projected over the crick.

I'd spread out my sweater, take a crunchy apple or a candy bar from my pocket, open a book, and settle in for an hour or two of bliss.

Cattle grazed beside me, the water bubbled below me and crickets chirped nearby. Sometimes a field of new-mown hay would send its fragrance on the breeze. Tasseled corn rustling in another field gave promise of the harvest to come.

Amid all that beauty, I'd immerse myself in a book about the wonderful world of places far from my rambling little crick.

But no place will ever be as wonderful as that little stream, the center of my summer world. I go back there often in my mind!

Larry Ulrich

Take a Leisurely Drive Past Some Beautiful Barns

IF YOU took that barn out of the picture above, the scene wouldn't be nearly as pretty. Likewise, it's the huge Pennsylvania barn, with its friendly "hex" signs and multipaned windows, that draws your eye to the photo at upper right.

No doubt about it, there is something about a barn that warms a heart as well as whatever's inside. They've become nostalgic symbols of simpler days.

Other than the Amish, few farmers build "barns" anymore, which have a haymow on the second floor to store forage. But most hay isn't handled in loose fashion

today, so new structures are more likely to be of a longer, lower, single-story design.

In a way that's unfortunate, because these new "box-like" buildings lack the character of earlier barns, which told you as much about a farmer or rancher as today's bumper stickers tell about the person behind the wheel.

As evidence, take a drive with our photographers through the next few pages. You'll learn that each ethnic group and each area of the country had its own style of barns...and each was warm and beautiful in its own special way.

RUSTY ROOF shelters barn on an old homestead site, above left, at North Pole Peak in Colorado's San Juan Mountains.

HEX SIGNS decorate many Pennsylvania Dutch barns, like the large one above. Symbols include stars, sun and flowers.

RAINBOW ROOFS, such as the one on this dairy barn in Trempealeau County, Wis., were designed to add loft storage.

DAZZLING OCEAN makes a beautiful backdrop, far right, for well-kept barn on ranch near Gull Rock and Sonoma, Calif.

37

Larry Ulrich

Jane Gnass

WEATHERED BARN stands amid the lush farm country of Illinois' Jo Daviess County, above, offering a silent but vivid reminder of bygone days.

CLEAR WATER in farm pond at upper left reflects the crisp contours of green-roofed barn located in the heart of northeastern Ohio's Amish country.

FINE MIST descends on distinguished older barn in Humboldt County, Calif., far left. Note nearby tree that apparently grew *around* the fence post!

GAMBREL ROOF and cupola add charm to barn, center left, in awesome setting before Chugach Mountains in Alaska's Matanuska Valley area.

CRIB BARNS, with tall center and "wings" on side, such as one at left, are common in Texas and the Southwest. This one is located near Boulder, Utah.

AFTERNOON SUN casts long shadows, above, as covered hack approaches barn with "cat slide" roof in Amish area of Berlin, Ohio.

UNUSUAL STRUCTURE in the scenic San Juan Islands of Washington, below, was obviously designed to accommodate steep slope.

ROUND BARN at left in Centre Co., Penn. has 16 "sides". Only stone, brick or tile barns were truly round. To make wood barn round required too much shaping of siding.

MORNING LIGHT glows on barns in Brown County, Indiana in top photo. Above, road winds around blue-roofed barn at Ontario, Wis.

TURN THE PAGE for a soothing scene as the sun begins to set on a majestic barn and wood fence in LaSalle County, Illinois.

Terry Donnelly

41

A Salute to the 4th!

INDEPENDENCE DAY is an old-fashioned, country kind of holiday, filled with flags, fireworks, parades and family gatherings. It's a time to reflect on our roots, our cherished freedoms and the hard work of the settlers who shaped our nation.

It's also a time to take pride in America. Hearing the National Anthem or seeing Old Glory in the summer breeze can sometimes bring a lump to the throat, but never more so than on the Fourth.

As you savor summer in the country, take time to reflect on just how lucky we are to live in "the land of the free and the home of the brave"!

Susan K. Bauer

Flag, Food and Fellowship Filled Old-Fashioned Fourth

By Carl W. Gregory
Higgins Lake, Michigan

The "Roaring 20s" were prosperous years for some, but for those of us who were farming then, they were as tough as ever. That made our holidays seem even more special, because on holidays, work was put aside.

We enjoyed all the holidays, of course. But our favorite was July 4th.

It was a patriotic holiday, a day to fly the flag. The Fourth meant family reunions, parades, firecrackers, fiddle music, lemonade, homemade ice cream ...and a big picnic.

Father, feeling somewhat uninhibited on this special day, decorated our old Model T with red, white and blue crepe-paper streamers that fluttered in the wind as we headed to the picnic grounds. He'd slowly ease down the gas level on the steering post until the old flivver reached 30 miles an hour, then 35!

Mother, holding firmly onto the door, shouted to be heard above the wind, "Hold your horses! Let's get there in one piece!" Father smiled as he eased up at the picnic grove.

The grove, on the shores of a small lake, was starting to fill up, with neighbors and friends staking out spots shaded by big elms near the water pump. Music floated over the grove as a fiddler practiced country tunes.

The women were busy arranging food on the tables, already piled high with picnic baskets and ice cream freezers. The men stood in groups, eyeing the horseshoe pits or talking about their crops and the weather.

"You get any of that rain over your way last week?" asked one farmer in blue serge trousers with wide black suspenders over his best white Sunday shirt.

"Nope," another replied. "Went right around us. We're dry as powder. But I heard they got a good soaker over by Butternut."

Soon it was time to eat—and what a feast! Each woman was counted on to bring her specialty, plus an assortment of sandwiches. One lady said to set the best table in the county brought her famed raspberry-filled four-layer cake topped with walnut-studded chocolate frosting.

Following the meal, we children would swim in the lake—but only after

"*M*usic floated over the grove..."

waiting an hour to prevent "cramps". The smaller children were admonished by their mothers not to go into water deeper than their belly buttons.

In the afternoon, a baseball game between neighboring towns was the big attraction. Unlike the usual pickup game, this one featured players in uniforms—and even an umpire!

In the evening there were fireworks, but we never stayed for that part. We went home early to set out cabbage plants. Many believed that the powder in the air from all those fireworks would trigger a nighttime thunderstorm—perfect conditions for growing cabbage.

We did have some fireworks of our own, though. Just before dusk, Grandfather always showed up with a big box full of cartwheels, Roman candles and giant sky rockets. Our private celebration lit up the sky.

At bedtime, far in the west, there were flashes of lightning. And as we drifted off to sleep, we wondered if maybe, just maybe, there was something to that old superstition.

Maybe we'd get a soaker just like the one over by Butternut!

Paulette McGriff

45

An Amish Barn Raising Is Something to See!

EVEN those Amish children in the foreground—who likely have become accustomed to this sort of thing—are fascinated with the organization, craftsmanship and the *speed* of an Amish barn raising.

They don't have the benefit of television and videos to have seen the sped-up development of a flower coming into bloom or a helium balloon being filled, but the process must seem quite similar as they watch how quickly a barn like this goes up—there was no more than a foundation here after breakfast and this crew put the roof on this barn before the noon lunch!

According to Doyle Yoder, who took this picture and lives in Holmes County, Ohio, the world's largest Amish community, around 700 men helped with this barn raising on the Wayne Burkholder farm near Farmerstown, Ohio. The barn was built to replace one that burned down 2 weeks earlier after being struck by lightning.

The men began arriving in buggies (imagine the sight of all those buggies!) at 6:30 in the morning. At that point, the cement-block foundation was laid and the concrete floor had been finished by a crew a few days earlier. That's all—all the wooden walls, purlins and rafters you see at right in this midmorning photo were put up in just a few hours after that early-morning start!

Meanwhile, the Amish women were preparing a huge meal for all those workers—many had brought "side dishes", homemade bread and desserts with them in their buggies. The meal consisted of big pots full of chicken and beef, mashed potatoes, garden vegetables, assorted pies and pitchers of lemonade. The lunch was served cafeteria-style and the workers sat on wagons, buggy hitches, machinery and the farm lawn, eating picnic-style.

When you consider this project required the organization of 700 workers, each with an assigned task, you're apt to be just as impressed as these Amish youngsters!

S now in Summer

*Majestic Mount Bachelor—a formidable
favorite of skiers and hikers—forms a
breathtaking backdrop to the dense
evergreens and tranquil Todd Lake near
Bend in central Oregon. Rugged mountain
beauty and forests that cover almost
half the state attract millions of
visitors to Oregon each year.*

Bob Clemenz

Join Us on a Tour of the Country's Most Magnificent Mills

THERE'S something soothing about an old mill. There just is. As evidence, take a stroll with us down by some old mill streams.

Study the scenes here and on the following pages...and *listen*.

You can almost hear the water pouring off that chute above... and there, did you pick up the creak and groan of the water-wheels of the other mills...and the exciting babble of the tumbling current at near right, as it races away—free again—after being captured and used by that seclud-ed red mill in the background?

Yet, in days gone by, these old

Ken Dequaine

Carr Clifton

Ken Dequaine

SOFT SUNLIGHT (upper left) casts a glow on the weathered wood of this well-kept gristmill at Guildhall, Vermont. Early mills were often neighborhood gathering places.

SUN-BLEACHED walkway leads to the Cable Mill in Cades Cove, Tennessee (above). This 19th-century structure still turns its huge millstone today with little maintenance.

mills were valued more for service than scenery. As wheat production spread across the country in the 1800's, so did the number of these functional mills for grinding feed and flour.

Even then, though, on lazy summer days, sitting, seeing and listening down by the old mill stream was likely medicinal.

As technology advanced, old mills and their wooden waterwheels gradually became obsolete. But thanks to caring people who preserved the ones shown here, we can appreciate their role in history...and remember.

RUSHING STREAM hurries below mill near Bakersville, North Carolina (left). This scenic spot is close to the Blue Ridge Parkway.

STONE GRISTMILL near Sudbury, Massachusetts (above) serves as a testimonial to the sturdiness of early 1900's construction.

Jerry Irwin

Willard Clay

Jerry Irwin

Willard Clay

Carr Clifton

EARLY AUTUMN'S finery and venerable, often-photographed Mabry Mill (above) are reflected in placid waters in rural Virginia.

GREENERY SURROUNDS historic mill in Pigeon Forge, Tenn. (upper left). Gristmills were designed to *last*—as evidence, this one was built well before Civil War, in 1830!

HUGE WATERWHEEL framed by flowering bushes and lush summer foliage (opposite far left) adds a touch of nostalgia to the campus of Berry College in Rome, Georgia.

SECLUDED WOODS shade gristmill on Roaring Fork in Great Smoky Mountains National Park (left). Millponds often doubled as reservoirs for rural fire fighting.

BUILT TO LAST in 1798 and treading water for a century and a half in Big Valley, Tennessee, the wood and stone mill at right was relocated to Norris Dam State Park in 1935.

Jerry Irwin

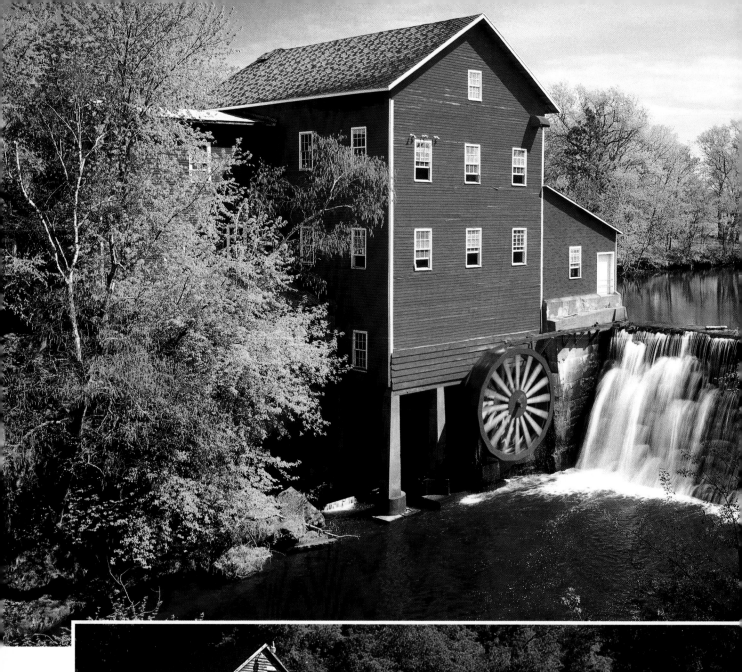

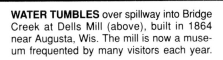

Ken Dequaine

Laatsch-Hupp Photo

WATER TUMBLES over spillway into Bridge Creek at Dells Mill (above), built in 1864 near Augusta, Wis. The mill is now a museum frequented by many visitors each year.

HYDE'S MILL (left) is one of the Midwest's few remaining mills powered by a wooden waterwheel. Built way back in 1850, it has been fully restored by its millwright owner.

JAEGER MILL (upper right) is located on Wisconsin's Crawfish River. Area elders say stones held up mill's original wooden dam.

ROMANTIC BEAUTY of the Jenny Grist Mill in Plymouth, Massachusetts (right) welcomes residents and tourists who come to enjoy scenery of the Cape Cod Bay area.

TURN THE PAGE to see cascading waters from wheel of a gristmill tumbling into Glade Creek in Babcock State Park, West Virginia.

Bob and Suzanne Clemenz

Ted Laatsch

Laundry Day Awash With Simple Pleasures

Few tasks in our daily routine offer the same sense of quiet satisfaction as hanging out the laundry.

By Darlene M. Seegert, West Allis, Wisconsin

I remember seeing Mom, her apron soaked from sloshing laundry in the washtubs, standing on the back porch and staring at a farmyard full of clothes on the line.

"Why is she looking at the clothes?" I wondered back then. Today, I find myself doing the same thing.

Sure, hanging out the wash is more work than tossing accomplished. There's personal pride and satisfaction in standing back and taking a long look at what I've done.

Mom obviously had the same affliction. She took pride in her clothesline, too, and hung everything out with methodical precision. She'd always hang like items together—you'd *never* see washcloths mixed in with un-

Jill Ransom

it in the dryer. So why do I do it? Mainly for the sweet, clean smell of clothes that have just been taken off the line. It's also an excuse to be outside, to study the sky and clouds and feel the sun and the breeze. It's good exercise, too!

But washdays aren't always idyllic. Gale winds can leave your favorite blouse on the ground, or tangle your sheets around the washline. Sometimes, after you've pinned up the very last sock, rain will come from out of nowhere. (Of course, if you take everything inside, the sky will be clear again 10 minutes later!)

Even with those hazards, seeing clothes on the line is important to me—it's a means of measuring what I've derwear! Darks and lights were hung separately, and all the socks faced the same direction in orderly rows.

I can still hear the Monday-morning chugging of Mom's wringer washer. She used a 3-foot broom handle to fish clothes from the bottom of the machine, since the water was so hot she couldn't put her hands in it. The thought of washing clothes in cold or even lukewarm water would have appalled her!

Doing laundry is much simpler now; these days, you don't even need to get your hands wet! But hanging out the wash is one tradition I refuse to abandon. Clothes dryers may be fine for some, but I'd rather be "hanging out" in my backyard, watching the clothes flutter in the breeze.

Country Morning

By Helen Wynn, Macon, Georgia

We country children always knew
Where blackberry bushes and wild plums grew.
So early on a summer day,
When none of us knew what to play,
With big straw hats and old lard pail
We'd set off on a sandy trail.

We picked till hands were scratched, and dye
Purpled our fingers; then the sun was high,
And our bucket was full; time to go back
Down the long, grassy wagon track.

We ate our plums both sour and sweet,
Then hawked our berries along the street
Ten cents a quart…but no one would buy.
So Mom bought them all—and made us a pie!

Take a Break from the 'Dog Days'!

The "dog days" of summer have arrived, bringing sultry days and humid nights. The afternoon rays seem to hug us close—even the air itself has a warm, rosy glow.

Don't let the heat get you down —savor this scene by imagining cooling your heels—and toes—in the still water, while watching the sunlight slip across the mountain.

Carr Clifton

Hunt for Treasure Had Happy Ending

When an old farmer befriended a young child, he helped the boy discover a treasure far greater than gold.

By Jimmy Lumpkin
Upland, California

Bob Firth

WHEN I WAS 7, Dad bought 160 acres of bottomland in Texas, near the forks of the Nueces and Frio Rivers. We'd no sooner climbed down from the wagon than we saw a stoop-shouldered old man with a face that could've been carved from the bark of an oak.

"Howdy, folks," he greeted us, taking off his leather cap. "My name is Carl Franzie. I live over there." He pointed to the big farmhouse across the railroad tracks.

After we shook hands all around, Mr. Franzie helped us unload the wagon, gave us some homemade bread, butter and hot coffee, and invited us to stop by his place.

My folks were pretty busy the next day, so I decided to visit Mr. Franzie. His farm was the most beautiful I'd ever seen, with a large vegetable garden, fruit and nut trees, and a vast field of cotton extending all the way to the oaks along the river.

Mr. Franzie was a widower, and he loved sharing his farm's beauty and having visitors—even if it was just a child like me. I began to visit him often.

One day, as we sat rocking in his porch swing, he told me about the treasure. He moved close to make sure I was listening; his eyes narrowed, and his voice became deep and intense.

"It was a long time ago," he said, "when Texas and Mexico were at war. General Santa Ana's army retreated from San Antonio with a cannon filled with gold. They decided to bury the treasure and come back for it later, but they lost the war and never had a chance to retrieve the gold. It's still there, waiting for someone to find it.

"I saw the cannon barrel once, sticking out of the riverbank down by the forks. Before I could dig it up, a flood carried it off and buried it again somewhere downstream. But someone will get it one of these days."

Started to Search

That very afternoon, I carried a hoe to the river and started digging. I was still at it that evening, when Mr. Franzie came along to check his fishing lines. He asked what I was doing.

"Looking for the treasure," I said.

He seemed surprised. "No, no, you'll never find it that way," he said. "Wait for a flood, and when the water goes down, watch for signs, like a chain or a wheel. Let the river show you where to dig."

I watched year after year, and though the river never did reveal to me the cannon's secret hiding place, I'd found a friend in Mr. Franzie. As the years passed, he patiently taught me how to swim, fish and hunt. No matter how busy my chores kept me, I always found time to spend with Mr. Franzie —and to look for the treasure.

Finally Dad bought another farm farther away, and I didn't see Mr. Franzie much anymore. I almost forgot about the treasure.

The last time I saw Mr. Franzie was when I came home from college at Easter. I found him lying asleep in the porch swing; for a long time I looked down into his weather-beaten face, remembering all the love and kindness he'd shown me.

Then he opened his eyes, blinked, and smiled. "You find the treasure?" he asked, sitting up. He extended his hand, which I gripped tightly as I sat down beside him.

"Yes," I nodded. "As a matter of fact, it was here all along. You showed it to me many times. I just didn't recognize it until now."

PASSAGE OF TIME CAN'T DAMPEN MEMORIES OF OLD SWIMMIN' HOLE

By R.S. McClurg
Fort Dodge, Iowa

The old swimmin' hole of my youth was a special place—a scene so tranquil it could've been plucked from the pages of a storybook.

In our tiny Iowa farm town, the "swimmin' hole" was a pond, formed when the gravel quarry was abandoned years before. Despite its humble origins, it was a delightful place. Emerald grass surrounded the water, which looked like a glittering sapphire sprinkled with diamond chips.

On the hottest days, the air was always filled with laughter, shouts and shrieks. The water was a jumble of swimmers playing games and floating on fat inner tubes and beach balls. Swimmers were free to come whenever they wanted—there was no closing time, no fence, no locked gate, no admission fee.

Almost everyone in town learned to swim in the old quarry pond. And we all participated in a certain amount of mischief there, too. Virtually every girl in town had been thrown into the water fully clothed, and almost every boy had gone skinny-dipping in the dead of night at least once!

There was nothing more delicious than swimming in the pond on a sizzling summer day—unless it was swimming there on a hot summer night.

As you approached the pond in the stillness of dusk, the heavy night air brimmed with humidity, the aroma of fresh-mown hay and the racket of croaking frogs. No feeling could quite compare with easing your weary body into that cool, refreshing water streaked with moonbeams and studded with starlight.

The swimmin' hole had been prepared for our use—we even had a lifeguard—but left as natural as possible. To get there, you had to take the old gravel road or the dirt footpath that wound through an untamed meadow where butterflies floated and bumblebees hovered over rainbow-hued wildflowers.

A pair of red brick bathhouses stood near the water, their gleaming white shutters and doors always as fresh as if they'd just been painted. Lilac bushes hugged the back of the women's bathhouse, and sweet clover dotted the lush grass surrounding it.

Stately oaks and maples shaded three picnic tables, a lopsided merry-go-round and a squeaky swing set. A cluster of rustling cottonwoods provided a canopy over a row of neat white benches. Sunbathers could stretch out on the grass or the cement "deck" near four wide steps leading into the water.

The steps were enjoyed by people of all ages. Teenagers sprawled on them in the sun, young parents used them to introduce their babies to the soothing water, grandparents soaked their feet while applauding the efforts of their grandchildren.

This past summer, I stood on those steps again. The pond hadn't been a swimmin' hole for at least 30 years, when the town fathers built a modern new pool on the far edge of town. I wanted to see how things had changed, and let my mind wander back to those wonderful days.

I found the pond surrounded by a chain-link fence. Many of the trees had been cut down; a new ball dia-

> ### *"No feeling could quite compare with easing into that refreshing water..."*

mond and playground had been built, and the cottonwoods had been replaced by a parking lot.

But some things hadn't changed. The shimmering water still glistened like a sapphire, and the lilac bushes were in bloom. Cattails waved in a swampy area near the water, and cottonwood seedlings had sprung up along both sides of the gravel road. Lush grass, thick bushes and wildflowers grew unhindered.

I walked to the water's edge, saddened that there are fewer and fewer of us who remember the charming times of yesteryear. But as I gazed at the wide steps, now cracked with age, I wondered if future generations would someday question why these cement steps descended into the water.

Wouldn't it be wonderful if they came up with the idea that the pond would be the perfect place to swim?

New Barn Built to Look Old

PASSERSBY look at George Smith's barn and likely figure it was built in the late '40's or early '50's. That pleases George greatly, even though the barn is scarcely a year old.

While some might wonder why anyone would want to build a new structure that looks decades old right after its completion, George and his wife, Myrna, had some good reasons for wanting exactly that effect. You see, when they set out to build this barn on their country acreage in the Blue Ridge Mountains of Haywood County, North Carolina, they were after an "authentic look".

Originally South Florida residents, George and Myrna felt the Blue Ridge region still held dear the old values. And George wanted to preserve for his grandchildren the things that he enjoyed as a boy—things like an old barn with all its nooks and crannies to hide and play in, filled with the fragrance of fresh-cut hay.

He remembered playing in an old barn like that when he was a kid. He enjoyed watching the barn swallows coming and going, and listening to the barn owl in early evening.

Rekindled Fond Memories

So, if he was going to build a new barn, it was going to be an old one! It was going to be one that fit in not only with other old barns in the area, but one that took him and his grandchildren back to those simpler times.

So began George's project and the search for the right materials to carry it off. The rusty tin roof, a must, was donated by a friend. The outside wood came from four separate buildings.

Some of the wood was donated, some bought, and some traded for.

Some of the doors and windows were donated, too, and those that weren't were handmade to match those of barns from the early '50's. New hinges for the doors were etched with muriatic acid to create the aged effect.

The hook and pulley at the top of the barn were found and purchased at a flea market. Locust poles to support the roof over the carport were cut from the Smiths' property.

'48 Truck Added Touch

After a month of sawing and hammering, George and his carpenter friend, Richard Balint, could stand back and imagine they were back in time, about 1948. So, to finish the effect, George went out and bought the '48 Ford truck shown in the picture.

The truck, fully restored, probably never had it so good, seeing as it's now sheltered by a carport next to a new/old barn with electricity, running water and a concrete floor stained to look like the surrounding soil.

Myrna's the one who insisted on the concrete floor, and George finally agreed to it, provided he could stain it to resemble Blue Ridge dirt. Myrna maintains that, had concrete been more accessible to people back in the early '50's, all barns would have had concrete floors.

Maybe so. What George does know is that he not only has a new barn that is in keeping with others in the area, but one that—each time he looks at it—takes him back to boyhood memories that, for him, are just as important to preserve as old barns.

Gene Ahrens

Monumental Meeting Place

Sculpted by centuries of wind, rain and sun, Independence Monument (center) and the surrounding striated sandstone mesas eerily occupy the Colorado National Monument between Fruita and Grand Junction. These steep-sided, flat-topped hills stand vigil along the state's western border in the Colorado Plateau. In contrast, flat, far-flung fields of green blend into a background of misty purple hills.

The Wanderer

Some people like a county fair
With exhibitions row on row.
Some like to travel highways where
The traffic whizzes to and fro.

But I prefer to follow trails
All dappled by the sun and trees
And see the birds on silver sails
Soar upward in the summer breeze.

I guess I'm just the fence-rail type,
A meadow rover seeking thrills
In finding berries purple-ripe
And listening to whippoorwills.

I like the sunset in my eyes,
The evening silence calm and deep,
When darkness curtains off the skies
And lulls the wanderer to sleep.

—*Herman T. Roberts, Hinsdale, Illinois*

Jack Jeffers

Turning Toward Home

By Wyn Thomas
Austin, Texas

Barbara Laatsch-Hupp/Laatsch-Hupp Photo

When we need our spirits strengthened and our sense of family restored, it's best to turn in one direction: Home.

It's always autumn in my memories of going home. The crisp, clear weather, red leaves and woodsmoke are part of returning to the fold.

This evening I'm taking my baby daughter, Meghan, home for the first time. "Home" is my grandmother's, a stone house on a graveled drive under century-old poplars and pecans. Here my mother, aunts, cousins and I gather each autumn in remembrance of our shared history and love for each other.

My mother, an aunt and I left at dusk for the long drive. Now, small towns unfold ahead of us as night falls. Winking lights spread across the dark miles, shadowing horses and cattle in the passing fields. Meghan sleeps with the intentness of babyhood, her fists curled with the effort.

Our turn looms suddenly in the dark, the first road past the cemetery. It's just as I remember it, stony and rough. The car crunches up the driveway where the porch light shines, and below it is my grandmother's face, anxious and waiting. She hurries to meet us, trying to see us all at once.

Quiet descends as I lift Meghan from her seat. Roused from sleep, she looks around foggily, then grins delightedly at my grandmother. I hand her over and they smile at one another, Meghan reaching to touch her cheek. It's a heart-tugging, memorable moment.

Inside, we settle around the table. Night closes in around us, sighing through the trees, as we talk late into the night.

I make my bed by the fire; when Meghan wakes, I will feed her by its light. As I flick off the last lamp, the light from the porch filters dimly into the room. This light burns always, a custom from my grandmother's youth, when it welcomed lonely and weary travelers. To me it still does.

Moments later, it seems, I awaken to the murmur of voices and the smell of freshly made coffee! I bundle up Meghan and we go out to greet the dawn from the porch steps. As I savor the sunrise and still-falling dew, she pats her quilt and coos at the leaves.

The others soon join us, sharing the steps and sunrise. All are quiet; some moments do not need words.

Beckoned by the smell of bacon, we go in for breakfast and find platters of food. My grandmother jokes that we come only to eat; with appetites raised by fresh country air, an observer would think she wasn't kidding!

The day is beautiful, cool and breezy, lit by clear, bright sunshine. Meghan rolls and tumbles across the yard, chasing skittering autumn leaves. The day has that curious quality that will make it a halcyon memory, magical and bright, with no discordant notes.

As twilight falls, we're drawn closer together. A quick hug and steady-eyed smile from my favorite aunt, usually so undemonstrative, bring me from my reverie. She feels it, too.

Supper conversation centers around family members, and there's a timeless feel as we talk. Tonight we're old and comfortable together.

Before, I've always come home as the granddaughter, the youngest, listening to others tell and retell our past. Tonight, the roles have shifted some. No longer just a listener, I'm now a mother and a storyteller, too.

The faces that greet my stories with gentle laughter are so much a part of what I value—character that is strong yet gentle. The years have held challenges for each of us, and I meet mine with the gift of this place and these people.

These gatherings are pilgrimages to our past and our present, and they give me strength. Tomorrow we'll return to our different lives. But tonight is to be shared and cherished.

A Blaze of Glory

The picturesque White Mountain National Forest is anything but white as autumn approaches. Even the white birch trees —a common beauty in New Hampshire— give off a golden glow while Mount Chocorua, one of the southernmost White Mountains, appears set on fire with its covering of blazing reds and fiery oranges. The vibrant colors reflect on the rippling waters of Lake Chocorua along the shoreline.

Fred Nieb

'Country Bumpkin' Learns to Grow Where He's Planted

The bright lights of the city don't hold much allure for a man who'd rather gaze at the stars.

By C. Robert Johnson, North East, Pennsylvania

Mrs. Charles Kota

When I was growing up, my friends sometimes talked of the day they'd be old enough to leave rural life behind and go to the big city. There was more to see and do there, they said—buildings tall enough to dwarf the county's largest dairy barn, lights so bright they dimmed the stars' brilliance, and "night life" that lasted till sunrise.

I assured my friends I wasn't impressed by skyscrapers or bright lights, and that my roots were just fine where they were planted.

The next thing I knew, I was looking for a job, and the first offer was in the city. So there I was, a "country bumpkin" smack in the middle of urban life. I couldn't believe all the people, cars, buildings…and concrete!

How could I possibly take root in a city where the topsoil was covered with a layer of cement? But jobs back home were scarce, so I decided to make the best of it.

Just as my friends had said, many of the buildings were big and attractive, designed by great architects and built with skilled hands to withstand the elements. But they also isolated their occupants from Mother Nature's kindness—many were so tall and wide that they blocked out the sun and the breeze.

The bright lights were there, too—bright enough that I needed sunglasses even after midnight! How could I enjoy a starlit evening when the stars were swallowed up by a sea of floodlights?

It didn't take me long to learn about "night life", either. It was true that the lights never went out, but if I spent the night on the town, I'd probably wake up too late to hear nature's prelude to a perfect sunrise.

I quickly tired of speeding down concrete highways to work in concrete buildings with concrete planters and plastic plants. I longed to walk dirt roads, relax on the front porch and smell the freshly turned earth after a spring shower.

I needed clean country air, peaceful evenings under a starlit sky, a general store where the cashier knew me, and the kind of relationship with God that comes easier when you're surrounded by the simple things in life.

Two months later I was in a rental truck, heading back home. I took the scenic route, avoiding all but the smallest of towns when I stopped to eat or rest. I'd seen enough "city" to last a lifetime!

Like others before me, I had to be true to my roots and grow where I'd been planted. "Country bumpkins" don't grow just anywhere!

Indian Summer

How grand to go a-gypsying today,
The yellow leaves crinkly 'neath my feet.
In silhouette, I see a pine tree sway,
And the air with harvest smells is sweet.

The woods are hushed and still, but whispering leaves
Subdued communion with each other hold.
The golden sunshine swathes the golden sheaves,
And through the woods I tread a path of gold.

One golden day—a day to drift and dream,
Before the grasp of winter's iron hand.
But in my heart its joy will brightly gleam
Till spring comes back again to cheer the land!

—Elma Helgason, Portland, Oregon

The Colors of Autumn

The autumn leaves are falling fast,
Yellow and gold and red and brown;
They sway and skip and even waltz
Before they finally drift down.

And purple grapes, clustered on vines,
Glisten in their coats of dew.
I search the honkings in the sky
And see wild geese across the blue.

Just now a mockingbird has perched
Among red-cheeked apples on the tree.
And some still say there is no God?
They must not see the things I see.

—Ruby Singley, Columbia, Mississippi

Gay Bumgarner

Fruits of Final Harvest Fill the Heart

For many gardeners, tilling the earth feeds not just the body, but the soul.

By Susan Hauser, Puposky, Minnesota

Photo/Nats

THE WILDFLOWERS are gone. Only a few lone asters light the roadsides; a handful of staunch pansies grace the gardens. Trees have taken over the job of coloring our lives—maples flame, birches rival the gold of the sun, oaks simmer in rust.

We're glad to be outside for one more day, to work a little longer with our backs to the sky. When we're bent over the ground that way, life seems a little simpler.

Today we'll dig potatoes, the last harvest of the year. The squash already are rescued from the frost, lining the shelves and the sills and the floors around the wood-stove. The heat will harden their shells, and in 2 weeks they'll be ready for the long wintering-over.

Husband Bill and I walk slowly down to the garden, the potato fork and metal baskets rattling in the cart behind us. Unlike the squirrels that raid our bird feeders, we're in no hurry.

Our eyes wander over the marsh that separates our tree line from the one across the way. The sky invites our gaze, too, and our minds drift with the clouds.

The garden brings us back to reality; it's a wreck. The potato plants have shrunk with the cold, and we'll have trouble finding them among the pigweed and nettles that took over while we lost ourselves in other summer pleasures. But we find the beginning of a row and begin to dig.

Bill thrusts the fork into the ground, steps on the top cross-piece and lets his weight sink the tines deep into the earth. I grasp the base of the plant with both hands.

Bill pushes back on the fork handle. As the earth rises up, I pull on the stalk.

Potatoes tumble up and out of their dark cave. The dirt falls away as we set them in the basket. When the first basket's full, we leave it and start another. When we're done, the garden is dotted with old metal egg crates filled with spuds.

We sit on the edge of the cart and rest a while. This is hard work, and we're not young. In fact, pulling the cart up the hill will use the energy we have left, and some we don't have at all.

For a moment we wonder why we do this. There are only two of us to feed, and we've grown enough pota-toes for a growing family.

Then I rummage in the crate next to the cart and pick out a potato that fits the palm of my hand. I jiggle it, testing its weight. I pick out another, then another, and pull out the front of my shirt, making a basket.

These are the ones I'll use for tonight's soup. The skins are so delicate they'll come off with a light brushing. The flesh is so crisp it will crackle when the knife cuts into it.

After simmering in light cream, these potatoes will make today's gardening efforts worthwhile, and body and soul will be nurtured by the gift of this harvest fulfilled. It comes from a labor that has no price, and we'll know again why some of the things we get out of our garden are as much food for the soul as the body.

Get Set for Autumn's Annual Art Gallery—It's Awesome!

YOU CAN SAY what you want about the fresh beauty of Spring, the laid-back days of Summer, and the bright clean white of Winter, but few will disagree that Fall is the grandest season of all!

Actually, there's no other word for it—autumn's artistry is *awesome!* Its wide-ranging palette of vivid hues can take your breath away, with brush strokes ranging from bright and broad to subtle and soothing.

It's a time to get the kids in the car...pack a picnic lunch...and head for the country. When Nature puts on a seasonal spectacu-

MEDLEY OF MUSHROOMS, maple leaves and pinecones are colorful mix in Oregon's Willamette National Forest.

lar like this, it's a show that shouldn't be missed.

So set aside some time during the glorious autumn days to store up a few sights, smells and tastes (such as tangy apple cider). Take a walk through the woods...take time to sit on a stump and savor the moment.

The scenes here should get you started. Our photographers caught autumn pulling the shade on summer across rural America in so many beautiful ways.

So, take our armchair tour... then take a drive...and do it before autumn leaves.

74

CHURCH STEEPLE and housetops (left) peek out from lustrous fall colors surrounding the valley village of East Topsham, Vermont.

SUN BURSTS THROUGH forked tree dispersing its golden glow over colored hills as autumn morning arrives in New Hampshire.

JAGGED PEAKS (left) rise behind a wall of trees in Grand Teton National Park, Wyoming, as a man fishes in Snake River.

OUT ON A LIMB, a fox squirrel finds a safe spot to nibble on a nut—perhaps deciding whether to store it for winter or eat it now!

GILDED LEAVES (far left) float lazily down stream studded by large stones in Shawnee Forest near Bell Smith Springs, Illinois.

GRANDPA passes on the knack of tying up bunches of pungent onions before hanging them to dry. Behind him and grandson, his garden grows ripe with squash and corn.

BRIGHT BANDS of aspens (right) zigzag down San Juan Mountains behind abandoned homestead at Telluride, Colorado.

PUMPKIN PICKERS. The thought of carving jack-o'-lanterns puts a smile on one boy's face (below right), but his brother seems unsure he picked the right pumpkin! Or maybe he's wondering how they'll fit all those pumpkins into one little red wagon.

TREES TINGED in an early autumn embrace of yellow and orange (below left) surround village in East Orange, Vermont.

Larry Ulrich

David Stoecklein

Gene Ahrens

PURPLE HAZE and color-splashed trees flank haze-covered Hudson River (above) spanned by graceful Bear Mountain Bridge in the New England Upland of New York.

A QUIET PLACE (top left) to reflect is offered by pine trees pointing their own reflections into placid waters of Seventh Lake in New York's colorful Adirondack Mountains.

LOVELY LOWBUSH blueberry shrubs (left) turn red on rocky hills of Mount Desert Island, which is Maine's largest offshore island.

SPOOKY FACE of giant jack-o'-lantern (top right) doesn't keep this inquisitive child from checking out source of candlelight inside.

MELLOW, MEANDERING river (right) narrows near sandy shore, contrasting with tree-filled landscape and snow-capped Mount Washington near Conway, New Hampshire.

Larry Ulrich

Scott Spiker

Carr Clifton

Julie Habel

AROMATIC HARVEST. Satisfied gardener heads for the house with fresh onions. And when you turn the page, you'll see a Vermont farm in a spectacular autumn setting.

Fred Sieb

Bob Taylor

Memories Are Made of This

Sometimes the best gifts we can give our children are also the simplest ones.

THE SOUNDS in the oak trees that surround our house grow quieter as the season changes and winter approaches. There are fewer birds, and the squirrels rarely venture out, except to gather a few more acorns for their cache. It's a quiet time—and a memorable one.

The ground is thick with fallen leaves, no longer green but brown from all the mulch. This morning our small son and I walked across the pasture, out from under the oaks and into the pines that thicken the ridge south of us. There we could hear the wind sweeping over the top of the trees; we hadn't noticed it before.

Clouds were gathering; a storm was coming. The forest no longer seemed peaceful, but nervous, its pulse quickening as the storm approached.

The weather turned quickly, bringing ominous foretellings of the winter to come—first rain, then sleet, and finally snow. The tall oaks, their branches no longer fertile with the greenness of summer, shook in protest and agitation. Inside, it was warm and cozy; outside, the wind whipped across the meadow, assaulting the neatly stacked hay that stood against it like a fortress.

I wondered where the deer were, especially the buck we saw early this morning, near our old hand pump. His

By Page Lambert
Sundance, Wyoming

tall, slender neck and gracefully turned head were motionless in the early-morning light. He stared directly at us, his nose held high as his nostrils flared, trying to take in our scent.

Then he pivoted, turned and jumped in a single motion and was gone. I hoped he was nestled in the tall grass somewhere now, down low in a draw perhaps, where the wind couldn't reach him.

The wind reached our son, though. He'd gone out into the storm with his dad to investigate voices we'd heard at the top of the ridge. It was hikers; they hadn't realized nature would be rallying her forces this afternoon.

He came back cold, wet and in tears, not yet acclimated to this early-winter weather. But the kitchen was warm and fragrant with the smell of muffins and zucchini bread fresh from the oven. Dry jeans, dry socks and warm muffins helped dry his tears; I was glad I'd picked this day to bake.

When our son looks back on his childhood, will he remember any of these times with special fondness?

Until today, I'd never thought of myself as a maker of memories, but perhaps I should. We all provide memories for our children.

Maybe if we think about that more often, we'll give them memories that will forever remind them of the special blessings of country living.

Rural Perspective

In the city,
Horizon to horizon,
All one can see
Is what man has made.

In the country,
Horizon to horizon,
All one can see
Is what God has made.

Fiery Fall

The cozy red cabin nestled along
a rocky stream in Vermont seems to beckon
visitors to come in out of the chill, perhaps to
sit down to a plate of pancakes with
Vermont-made maple syrup!
The countryside presents a colorful
picture of orange-soaked sugar maples and other
trees, offset by a powdery purple sky.

Wood Stove's Glow Warms Hands and Hearts

It's often said that wood "warms you twice". This writer feels the warm memories kindled by a wood stove can last a lifetime.

By Rosa Hatfield, Mentone, Indiana

We have a wood furnace in our home. We think of it primarily as a great way to save on our utility bill—but mostly it's a great way of bringing back childhood memories.

We had a wood stove when I was a child, and there was nothing quite as comforting as warming up next to that glowing potbellied stove. You had to be careful not to get too close, though! Sometimes one of us would sit with our feet propped up too near it, and soon we'd smell our shoes scorching.

We learned there was a trick to staying evenly warm. You had to keep

> **"If I was upset about something, chopping wood usually made me forget about it..."**

turning, because while one side of your body was feeling scorched, the other side would be freezing!

The wood stove was a great place to hang your laundry to dry, too—as long as you waited until everyone else went to bed. Otherwise, someone was sure to inadvertently push the chair a little closer to the stove. Of course, it seemed no one would ever notice until the garment hanging on the back of the chair started to smoke. I lost several sweaters that way!

It was my job to split wood and cut kindling for our stove, and I enjoyed it —both because I liked outdoor chores and because it was a great way to work off youthful anger. Many times I was out chopping wood when we didn't even need it!

If I was upset about something, chopping wood for an hour usually

Doris Gehrig Barker

made me forget about it. Even when I didn't forget, the problem never seemed as important afterward.

I even had a favorite wood stove— the one Grandma cooked on. To my young eyes, this stove was a wonder. If something needed to be cooked quickly, you just moved it over to the hottest part, near the front.

Grandma cooked entire meals on the stove at once, and her food—especially her biscuits and corn bread—

was the best that I've ever tasted.

Today, whenever I fire up our wood furnace, all those memories return. This new wood furnace is a back-up heat source, not our only one as it was during childhood.

The furnace doesn't look much like the stove I remember, either. But I appreciate it just as much. Somehow, our house seems warmer when it's being heated by the glow that only a wood fire can provide.

Sneak Peek Amid Peaks

AUTUMN'S still in the air, down below, but high up in the mist-shrouded Rockies —where Willard Clay climbed to take this late fall photo— the evergreens are already wearing a light coat, giving us all a sneak preview of days soon to come.

You can almost *hear* how quiet it is...and *feel* the solitude high up in these isolated mountains. Thanks, Willard, for taking us there.

*B*undle *U*p and Join *U*s to Witness Winter's Wonders!

BUTTON UP your overcoat, grab a cap and mittens, and pull on your boots...it's time to get outdoors for a close-up look at a crisp winter wonderland!

Choose a day when it's not too cold—maybe a bright, sunny morning just after a snowfall—and hike or drive to a spot that will let you fully appreciate the season's beauty undisturbed.

There's a profound, almost reverent silence right after a snowfall that's...well, soothing. We may complain about the cold weather that winter brings, but then who among us hasn't been moved by the sight of a fresh, deep, fluffy blanket of snow unmarked by a human's touch?

Think about it—weren't there a few mornings last winter when you peeked out the window for a routine check of the weather and found yourself startled by the beauty outside...so much so that you caught your breath?

Winter is full of such surprises. And if you don't want to venture outdoors or "up North" to appreciate them in person, just find a cozy chair—our roving photographers have brought you plenty of spectacular scenes to share!

CHERUBIC CHILD hikes through fresh snow in Kalamazoo, Michigan. Looks like she's already made a few "snow angels"!

W. Pote/H. Armstrong Roberts

Terry Donnelly

GLOWING STEEPLE on church in the heart of quaint New England village (left) beckons local townspeople for Christmas services.

SNOWSHOE TRAIL winds along solitary but inviting route through pines near Cottonwood Creek in Chaffee County, Colorado.

SNOW-CAPPED BRIDGE is a favorite of photographers all year long near Franconia Notch in central part of New Hampshire.

ICE-DRAPED BRANCHES hang suspended over a creek in the Hoover Wilderness, deep in California's Sierra Nevada mountain range.

Larry Ulrich

Fred Sieb

89

Carr Clifton

ROSY-RED BERRIES add a vibrant burst of color to wintry landscape (upper left) near peaceful-looking farm in Connecticut.

TRAPPER'S CABIN is surrounded by high-country splendor (far left). This remote cabin is perched on edge of Engineer Mountain, in Colorado's scenic San Juan mountain range.

FAT SNOWFLAKES flutter around a pair of isolated horses (left) trudging toward shelter in Oregon's Columbia River Gorge area.

SHAFTS OF SUNLIGHT paint hillside at Indian Creek, California with a dazzling swath of gold (above). Fascinating scene is in northern Sierra Nevada mountain range.

WESTERN-STYLE holiday charm envelops main street of Crested Butte, in Gunnison County, Colorado (at right). That's Mount Crested Butte looming in the background.

Steve Terrill

Terry Donnelly

Greg L. Ryan

Grant Heilman

92

WARM SUN melts previous days' snowfall near Rosedale, Illinois (above). You can "hear the quiet" as farmers along winding road enjoy winter's slower pace.

INNER TUBE takes two youngsters on a rollicking ride down a snow-slicked hillside in rural area of northern Minnesota (far left).

EVERGREEN SPIRES rise majestically, stretching their snow-capped limbs up toward the azure sky against a mountainous backdrop in the heart of northwestern Colorado (left).

Carr Clifton

PINK-TINGED CLOUDS streak the sky as sun slowly sets on Indian Creek (above right) in California. This unspoiled area lies within the northern range of Sierra Nevada Mountains.

TURN THE PAGE for glittering scene one of our photographers captured in Colorado's San Juan National Forest. Notice how snow glistens on aspens and blue spruces? Peaks in background are Whitehead Mountains.

Larry Ulrich

A Shepherd Remembers...

This touching, true story from a Texas sheep rancher arrived the day after we'd finished this issue. When we read it, we retrieved this page from the printer and changed the copy—we just had to share it with you prior to the holiday season.

By Calvin D. Putnam
Merkel, Texas

IT SEEMS the Lord can still use humble shepherds in today's world. Let me tell you why.

I grew up on a Kansas sheep farm, where we raised registered Shropshire sheep for years. But during the drought and Depression of the 1930's, in dry, dusty Kansas, a lot of young people's dreams vanished like the sun did during daytime dust storms, as did the moon and stars at night.

The saddest thing I ever saw as a shepherd in those days was on a cold night I found a pair of twin lambs crying by the side of their dead mother. After taking in this sad scene, I got one lamb under one arm, then with some difficulty caught the other and got it under the other arm. I carried them to the sheepfold where I could see that they were bottled and fed. Still, I heard those orphans cry and it bothered me.

I was reminded of this later in life when we adopted our daughter "Demetra". She was born in a little mountain village in Greece, where there was no road into the village that a vehicle could travel on. They went to town on donkeys or a horse.

Demetra was 7 and her sister was 5 when their mother died. Their father was a shepherd. He was illiterate, because he was the youngest in the family and was needed to herd his father's flock, so he never got to school. Worse, he had heart trouble and was crippled, and couldn't take care of his little girls.

We adopted Demetra when she was

"LOST LAMBS" Sarah, at left above, and Rebecca, right, obviously love "shepherd", Calvin Putnam, who adopted them. Photo below was taken when they reunited in 1961.

placed with an adoption company in America. We met her in Dallas, Texas at Love Field on Feb. 17, 1959. She was 8 years old.

We lived in Arkansas then, and the first evening at our farm we had two bottle lambs for her to feed. She spoke only Greek and we spoke only En-

glish. As she fed the lambs, she smiled and said, "Demetra zagpe provts, baba." In English: "I love the lamb, Daddy."

Some time later she said, "Me got a sister in Greece somewhere, Daddy."

I asked, "You have a sister, Demetra?"

"Yes," she answered. "Will I ever see her again?"

I felt like a shepherd who had gotten one lamb under one arm and left the other out in the night alone with the coyotes. My wife and I realized we had no choice but to search for the lost lamb.

We learned she was in Tripoli in another home. But when contacted, their father in Greece wanted them reunited in our home in America. So, 29 months later, on July 7, 1961, the two sisters were reunited at O'Hare Field in Chicago.

Today they are both married and have children. Demetra is now Rebecca, and works in the office of four heart doctors. Her sister is now Sarah, and works at a hospital. They wanted American first names.

They both live in Abilene, Texas, so they are once again reunited in America. We wanted to share this story with you this Christmas season.

As I said, it seems the Lord can still use humble shepherds in today's world. I just didn't realize that back on that cold evening years ago, when I carried those twin lambs back to the sheepfold after their mother died.

Years Later, Mystery Still Lingers...

F. Sieb/H. Armstrong Roberts

*It's still the most unusual Christmas gift he's ever received...
and the years since haven't made it any less intriguing.*

By Richard A. Pence, Fairfax, Virginia

SOME MYSTERIES in life are sweeter when they remain just that—mysteries. Like the mystery surrounding my bicycle back when I was 12.

It was in the midst of World War II, and Dad had just returned from visiting friends and relatives in another part of the state. When he pulled up in front of the house, he hollered at me to help him unload the pickup truck.

To my delight, it included some precious cargo—a *bicycle*! For me! A dream come true!

To be sure, it was hardly a new one, but its former owner had little use for it, since he had grown and was now somewhere in the South Pacific.

But my ecstasy quickly turned to despair: The tires and tubes had long since succumbed to wear and weather. There weren't enough hot patches at the Standard station, or enough black friction tape at Uncle Milo's hardware store, to keep them inflated. With its flat tires, the bike was so hard to pedal that an hour or two of riding now and then was about all that I could manage.

Bicycles were hard to come by during the war, but getting tires for them was all the more difficult, if not impossible. A farmer might get a permit for two tires for his grain truck, but how could a 12-year-old get the go-ahead to buy a couple of bike tires? And that was assuming such tires even existed, which I had been assured was pretty unlikely.

Summer passed and so did fall, and most of the time the bike stood in the garage, unused and unusable. It was the cruelest of injustices—to have something, yet not have it.

That winter, on Christmas Eve, the whole family gathered to pass out and open the few presents we could find or afford. Suddenly we heard a sharp sound on the front porch.

"Santa Claus!" we kids shouted, dashing out.

We were right—and he'd left something there on the porch for each child. But my attention was riveted to one spot. There, hanging on a large nail by the door, still gently swaying, were two bicycle tires—*honest-to-goodness real rubber balloon tires!* Twenty-eight-inchers! With tubes! And brand-spanking new!

I stood there with my mouth open, wondering how Santa had managed such a feat—after all, those were probably the only two new bike tires in the whole United States! But I didn't ponder too long—every child knows Santa can do most anything he really wants to.

Years later, though, in a moment of special communication between father and son, I casually asked Dad if he knew how Santa had managed it. He grinned, paused, then just said he wasn't really sure.

I guess I'm just as happy today not knowing. The mystery keeps the memory so much sweeter.

The Lesson of the Christmas Rose

*Now and then it takes a small miracle to
show us the good in others is right before our eyes.*

By David C. Keller, Lancaster, Pennsylvania

MISS ELLY loved to scold. She scolded politicians, neighbors, the schools, deliverymen, repairmen, the weather and the Ladies Aid Society at church. Miss Elly scolded everything and everyone. Even me.

This was back in the 1940's in our little Pennsylvania town, and I was her paperboy.

"The paper's wet! It's wrinkled! Must be cheap ink—look at my hands!" I heard this every day—even on bright, fine days. Miss Elly scolded me day in and day out for the entire 7 years I knew her.

But could she grow flowers! Hers were the kinds of blooms that almost caused accidents. As they drove home from work, folks would slow down noticeably just to get a good look at her flowers.

Flowers completely surrounded her white wood house; in contrast to Elly's cantankerous personality, the whole place seemed to laugh and dance in the perfume of the multi-hued blossoms from spring through fall.

In winter, most of the women's and men's organizations—including some from out of town—took tours to Miss Elly's place to see her "Christmas collection" inside.

No one ever stayed too long, though, because Miss Elly was in a scolding mood even during the holiday season. "Wipe your boots!" "Look out—don't touch!" "All it takes is water and good care, don't you know that?"

I didn't see Miss Elly much after I gave up my paper route. I graduated from high school and left for college. Then, while I was home for the Christmas holidays during my freshman year, Miss Elly died.

I didn't want to go to the viewing—Miss Elly was only a memory now, and I had other plans for the night—but my mother insisted. "You owe it to her," she said gently.

The roads were coated with ice and snow as I drove to Corman's Funeral Home. I waited in line with the others in the vestibule, but when I finally got to see Miss Elly, I didn't recognize her. Only the drawn-down lines of her mouth stirred a memory.

Then I looked at her folded hands. Someone had put a flower there—a white Christmas rose in the prime of its life. Miss Elly's fingers curled gently around the stem. It was beautiful.

After signing the visitors' book, I walked to the door to greet Mr. Corman, who seemed a little distracted.

"Hi, Mr. Corman," I said. "Did you put that rose in Miss Elly's hand for the viewing tonight?"

His reply was slow and uncertain. "No," he said. "I checked the room before visitation began at 7 o'clock, and there was no rose there then. I saw it later, just after the viewing started, but it was just a bud. Now it's in full bloom. I have no idea how that rose got there!"

It was warm—almost hot—in the funeral home, and I suggested maybe the heat forced the bud to open.

"No, no," Mr. Corman said, shaking his head. "A rose won't bloom in 5 minutes. I know because I raise them. Not as well as Miss Elly did, though."

I looked back at the line of mourners and said wonderingly, "Well, Mr. Corman, Miss Elly always could grow flowers."

Later, I heard that at 9 o'clock, when the viewing ended, Miss Elly held four perfect white roses in her hands.

Miss Elly scolded everything...but she never scolded her flowers.